DINOSAURS CAN BE SMALL

Darrin Lunde • *Illustrated by* **Ariel Landy**

ini Charlesbridge

A **BRONTOSAURUS** raises its head above a ginkgo tree.

It is a long-necked dinosaur.

Brontosaurus (brawn-tuh-SAWR-us)

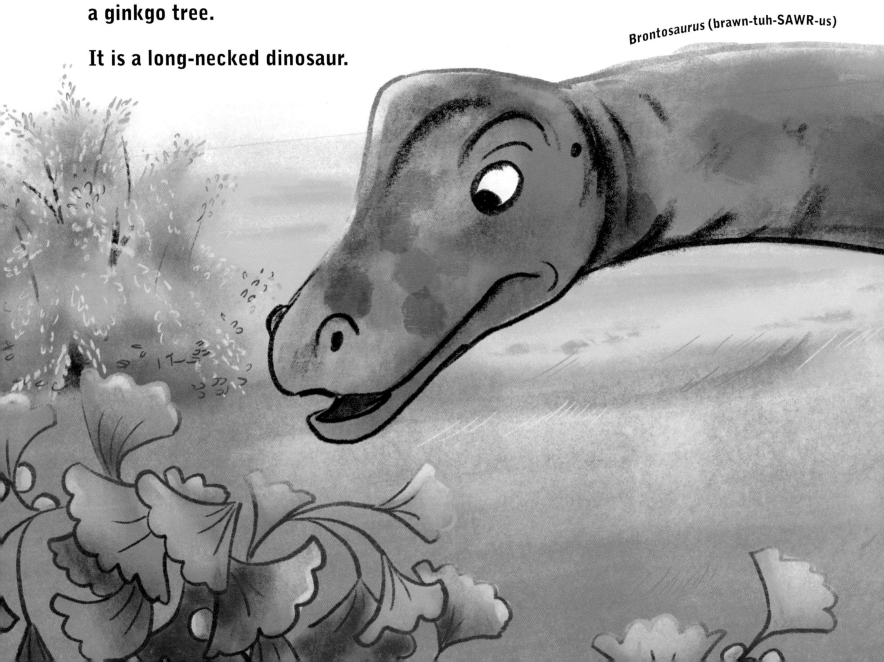

But not all long-necked dinosaurs are big.
Some long-necked dinosaurs are small.

MAGYAROSAURUS is one of the smallest long-necked dinosaurs.

It lives on an island where there is not much food to eat.

Magyarosaurus (mag-yar-oh-SAWR-us)

Magyarosaurus survives because it does not need to eat as much as the big dinosaurs.

Brontosaurus: 20 ft. tall, 80 ft. long
Magyarosaurus: 5 ft. tall, 20 ft. long

A **TRICERATOPS** pushes over a tree fern to eat.

It is a horned dinosaur.

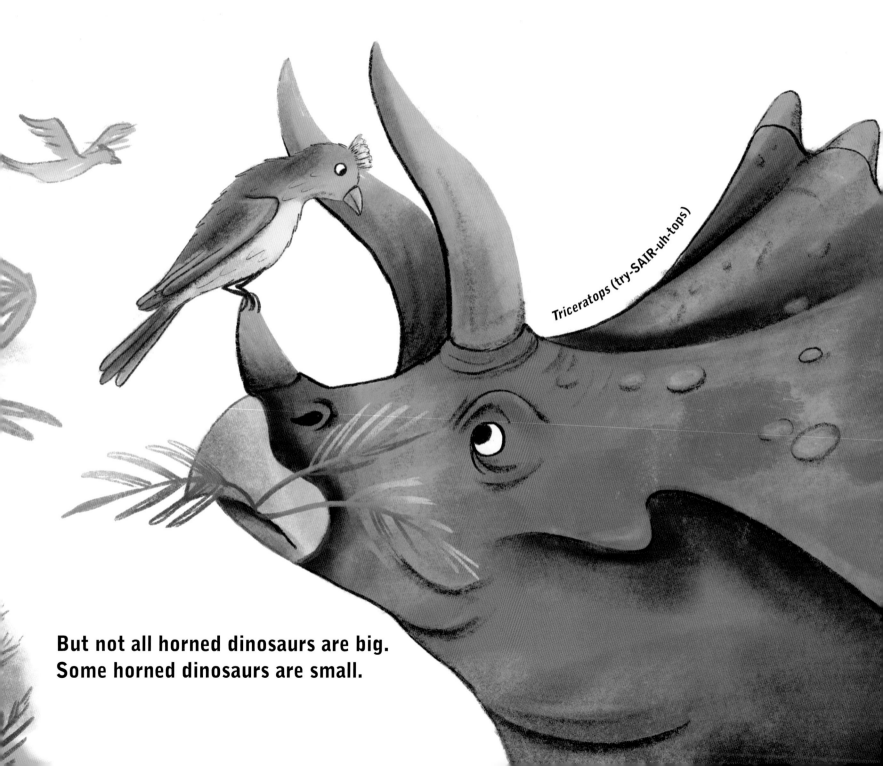

Triceratops (try-SAIR-uh-tops)

But not all horned dinosaurs are big.
Some horned dinosaurs are small.

MICROCERATUS is one of the smallest horned dinosaurs.

It has short front legs and walks on its two back legs.

Microceratus (my-kro-SAIR-uh-tus)

Microceratus is able to hide from big meat-eating dinosaurs because it is small.

Triceratops: 12 ft. tall, 30 ft. long
Microceratus: 15 in. tall, 2 ft. long

A **TYRANNOSAURUS** bites into a dead dinosaur with its six-inch-long teeth.

It is a meat-eating dinosaur.

Tyrannosaurus (tie-RAN-uh-SAWR-us)

But not all meat-eating dinosaurs are big.
Some meat-eating dinosaurs are small.

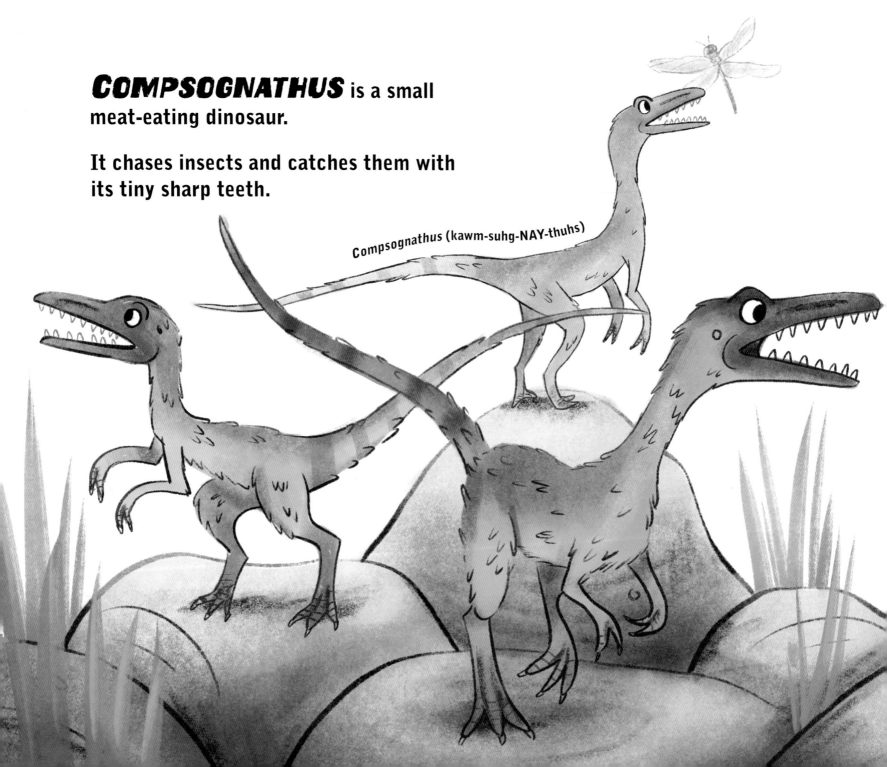

COMPSOGNATHUS is a small meat-eating dinosaur.

It chases insects and catches them with its tiny sharp teeth.

Compsognathus (kawm-suhg-NAY-thuhs)

Insect meat is very nutritious dinosaur food.

Tyrannosaurus: 12 ft. tall, 40 ft. long
Compsognathus: 10 in. tall, 2–3 ft. long

A **PACHYCEPHALOSAURUS** fights using its ten-inch-thick skull.

It is a dome-headed dinosaur.

Pachycephalosaurus (pak-ee-SEF-uh-lo-SAWR-us)

But not all dome-headed dinosaurs are big. Some dome-headed dinosaurs are small.

MICROPACHYCEPHALOSAURUS
is a small dome-headed dinosaur.

Micropachycephalosaurus may be small, but it has the longest name of any dinosaur.

Micropachycephalosaurus (my-kro-pak-ee-SEF-uh-lo-SAWR-us)

Tiny dinosaurs with big names get extra attention!

Pachycephalosaurus: 6 ft. tall, 15 ft. long
Micropachycephalosaurus: 16 in. tall, 3 ft. long

A **QUETZALCOATLUS** soars high above a *Tyrannosaurus.*

It is not a dinosaur but a close relative called a pterosaur (TER-oh-sawr).

All pterosaurs fly.

Quetzalcoatlus (ket-zel-KWAT-uh-lus)

But not all pterosaurs are big.
Some pterosaurs are small.

NEMICOLOPTERUS is a small pterosaur.

It is a good climber and hunts insects in the trees.

Big pterosaurs are too clumsy to climb trees.

Nemicolopterus (NEM-ee-kohl-OP-ter-us)

Quetzalcoatlus: 33+ ft. wingspan
Nemicolopterus: 10 in. wingspan

A **SHONISAURUS** swims through the ocean hunting fish.

It is not a dinosaur but a marine reptile called an ichthyosaur (IK-thee-uh-sawr).

All ichthyosaurs swim.

Shonisaurus (show-nee-SAWR-us)

But not all ichthyosaurs are big.
Some ichthyosaurs are small.

MIXOSAURUS is a small ichthyosaur.

It looks like a mix between an eel and a dolphin.

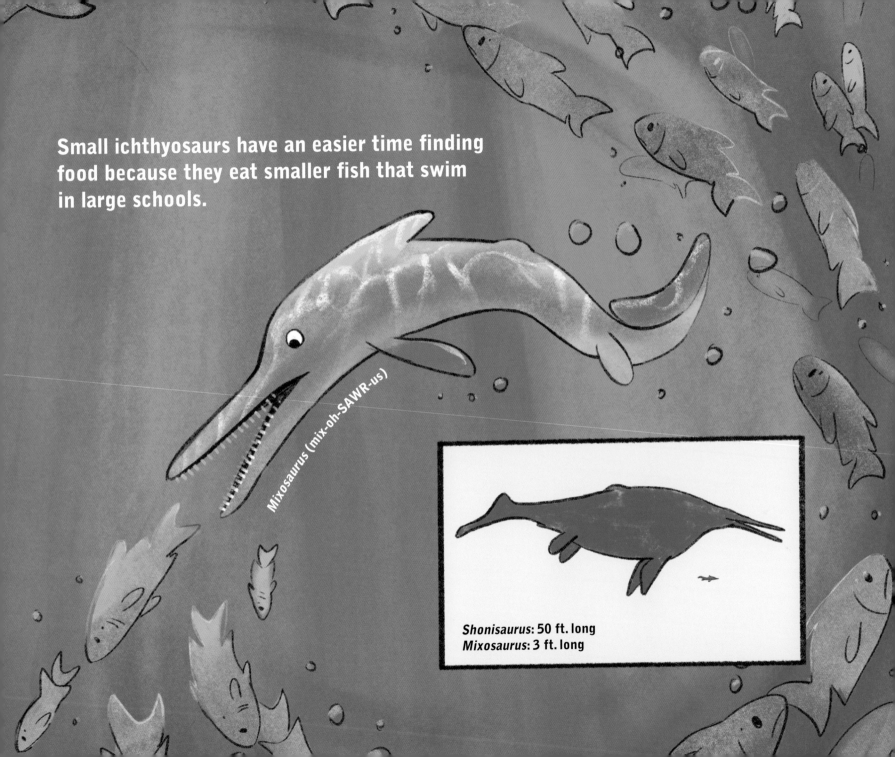

Small ichthyosaurs have an easier time finding food because they eat smaller fish that swim in large schools.

Mixosaurus (mix-oh-SAWR-us)

Shonisaurus: 50 ft. long
Mixosaurus: 3 ft. long

A huge fiery ball races through the sky, hurtling toward Earth.

It is a giant meteor!

A head peeks out from a hole in the ground.
It is a small dinosaur covered with feathers.

When a giant meteor hit Earth sixty-six million
years ago, the explosion turned the air red-hot for
several hours.

Only the smallest dinosaurs survived. Some
scientists think they survived because they could
hide underground, but nobody knows for sure.

These tiny survivors were dinosaurian birds, and they are still living today. Birds are the surviving members of a group that included all the dinosaurs.

Being big isn't everything.
It's sometimes very good to be small.

Here are the names of all the dinosaurs mentioned in this book.
Learning something about what their names mean will help you remember them.

BRONTOSAURUS

means "thunder lizard," from the Greek words *bronte* for thunder and *sauros* for lizard.

MICROCERATUS

means "small-horned," from the Greek words *mikros* for small and *keratos* for horned.

COMPSOGNATHUS

means "elegant jaw," from the Greek words *kompsos* for elegant and *gnathos* for jaw.

MICROPACHYCEPHALOSAURUS

means "small thick-headed lizard," from the Greek words *mikros* for small, *pakhys* for thick, *kephale* for head, and *sauros* for lizard.

MAGYAROSAURUS

means "Magyar lizard," from the Magyar tribes of people that settled in Hungary, where this dinosaur was found, and the Greek word *sauros* for lizard.

MIXOSAURUS

means "mixed lizard," from the Greek words *mixis* for mixing and *sauros* for lizard.

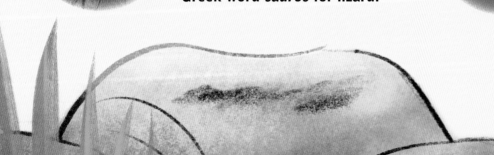

NEMICOLOPTERUS

means "forest-dwelling winged creature," from the Latin words *nemus* for forest and *cola* for dweller, and the Greek word *pteros* for feather or winged creature.

SHONISAURUS

means "Shoshone Mountain lizard," from the mountain range that was named for the Shoshone Native American tribe and the Greek word *sauros* for lizard.

PACHYCEPHALOSAURUS

means "thick-headed lizard," from the Greek words *pakhys* for thick, *kephale* for head, and *sauros* for lizard.

TRICERATOPS

means "three-horned face," from the Greek words *tri* for three, *keras* for horn, and *ops* for face.

QUETZALCOATLUS

is named after the Aztec feathered serpent god, Quetzalcoatl.

TYRANNOSAURUS

means "tyrant lizard," from the Greek words *tyrannos* for tyrant and *sauros* for lizard.

For Sakiko, small but mighty—*D. L.*

For Robin, the tall to my small—*A. L.*

Special thanks to Carl Mehling, Senior Museum Specialist in the Division of Paleontology at the American Museum of Natural History, and Mary Knight, Managing Editor at the American Museum of Natural History, for sharing their invaluable expertise and advice.

Published by Charlesbridge
9 Galen Street
Watertown, MA 02472
(617) 926-0329
www.charlesbridge.com

Printed in China
(hc) 10 9 8 7 6 5 4 3 2 1

Library of Congress Cataloging-in-Publication Data

Names: Lunde, Darrin P., author. | Landy, Ariel, illustrator.

Title: Dinosaurs can be small / Darrin Lunde; illustrated by Ariel Landy.

Description: Watertown, MA: Charlesbridge, [2024] | Audience: Ages 3–7 | Audience: Grades K–1 | Summary: "Dinosaurs are famous for being big, but some of the most interesting ones were small. Young readers compare six tiny dinosaurs with their massive counterparts and learn that being big isn't everything. Sometimes it's very good to be small."—Provided by publisher.

Identifiers: LCCN 2023029756 (print) | LCCN 2023029757 (ebook) | ISBN 9781623543303 (hardback) | ISBN 9781632893048 (ebook)

Subjects: LCSH: Dinosaurs—Juvenile literature. | Dinosaurs—Size—Juvenile literature. | Size perception—Juvenile literature.

Classification: LCC QE861.5 .L848 2024 (print) | LCC QE861.5 (ebook) | DDC 567.9—dc23/eng/20231102

LC record available at https://lccn.loc.gov/2023029756

LC ebook record available at https://lccn.loc.gov/2023029757

Illustrations done in digital media
Display type set in Bourough Grotesk Pro by Lewis McGuffie and Geoduck Regular by Stephen Miggas
Text type set in Bell Gothic Black by Chauncey H. Griffith
Printed by 1010 Printing International Limited in Huizhou, Guangdong, China
Production supervision by Mira Kennedy
Designed by Jon Simeon